Ministering Through Poetry

The Joy Behind The Smile

Gwyn G. Harris

Library of Congress Control Number: 2015934367

ISBN 978-1-62806-062-1

Published by Salt Water Media
29 Broad Street, Suite 104
Berlin, Maryland 21811
www.saltwatermediallc.com

Scripture quotations, unless otherwise noted, are taken from the New King James Version or the New International Version of the Bible.

Introduction

Ephesians 4:12

"…to equip his people for works of service so that the body of Christ may be built up."

I Corinthians 12:5

"There are different kinds of service but the same Lord."

When I started to write poetry I was far from thinking about God or thankfulness or finding salvation. Written during times of happiness, brokenness, heartache, loneliness or pain this art became a crutch and a personal escape route that helped me to cope, enhance my imagination and calm my fears. In an odd way I began to use this to not only better understand the world around me and myself but also to receive a semblance of spiritual healing. Through years of repetitiveness and practice I developed a knack for facing issues and in the process found that poetry indeed speaks to my heart. And thus, a compelling passion for writing was born.

The more I wrote the more I became entrenched and fell in love with the process. My level of ability has evolved over the years. Soon my poetry became a vital means of praise and thanks for the Holy Trinity. And writing is one way I communicate with that higher power.

I have come to appreciate my skill to be able to present words of faith through this vehicle of poetry as motivational gifts for both serving and teaching. Because of these I am in effect ministering in a nontraditional manner. It is my belief that writing is a purpose for my existence and was never intended to be solely for my entertainment but to be shared and as a platform by which I am able to serve an all-powerful and loving god.

As Christians we each have a responsibility to be witnesses and to serve. Let us not forget the following scriptures:

1 Corinthians 14:12 *"So it is with you. Since you are eager for gifts of the spirit try to excel in those which buildup the church."*

I Peter 4:10 *"Each of you should use whatever gift you have to serve others, as faithful stewards of god's grace in its various forms."*

II Corinthians 9:12 *"The service that you perform is not only supplying the needs of the Lord's people but is also overflowing in many expressions of thanks to God."*

Romans 12:6-8 *"Having then gifts differing according to the grace that is given to us, let us use them: if prophesy in proportion to our faith; or ministry, let us use it in ministering; he who teaches, in teaching; he who exhorts, in exhortation; he who gives, with liberality; he who leads, with diligence; he who shows mercy, with cheerfulness."*

ACKNOWLEDGEMENTS

I must give credit to the church in which I grew up and still attend and receive my spiritual teachings, St. James Free Methodist Church in Quantico, Maryland. I have benefited from instructions under the late Reverends Luther Stanley and Maynard Smith and the former pastor, Reverend Annette Wilson and the present pastor, Reverend Louis L. Reid Sr., the assistant pastor, Reverend Gloria Taylor Lewis and the assembly of associate ministers and members.

And of course there has been the support and encouragement I have received from my daughters, Genienne Elsey Walter and Genae Elsey and my husband, Chester Harris. Among my staunch supporters has been two fellow writers, Camella Ward, and author, Pastor Catherine Smith-Wooten, along with other family members and friends.

Because of Jesus Christ, the joy of Christian fellowship and hard work and dedication this dream has become a reality at last and I wish to thank you all.

DEDICATION

Foremost, this book is dedicated to the first two people I loved in life, my parents, Titus R. Gattis and Frances Tull Gattis. Their influence, nurturing and guidance became the building blocks which formed the person I am today. I am forever blessed and affected by their love which now flows from Heaven. And with pride I honor their memories and hail their legacies.

Several elementary school teachers taught me to read and write and because of them I started writing poetry at an early age and subsequently developed a passion for this art. They are now deceased. Their names are: Mrs. Mae Maddox, Mrs. Rose Barkley and Mrs. Harriet Ballard. I share my thanks with them as well.

And finally, I dedicate this book to my daughters, Genae Elsey and Genienne Elsey Walter, my grandchildren, Alexxus, Christian and Ryanne, my brothers Keith and Danny, and my husband, Chester Harris. Included in this dedication is the entire Gattis, Tull and Handy families located primarily on Maryland's Eastern Shore. Sending special love and appreciation to each one of you.

CONTENTS

CHAPTER 2: OVERCOMING ISSUES AND ADVERSITY

CHAPTER 3: A GENERAL ASSORTMENT OF POEMS

CHAPTER 4: THE SUBJECT OF DEATH AND POEMS THAT MEMORIALIZE

CHAPTER 1

FAITH, PRAISE AND ENCOURAGEMENT

✝

I Thessalonians 5: 16-18

"Rejoice always, pray continually, give thanks in all circumstances for this is God's will for you in Christ Jesus."

Hebrews 11:6

"And without faith it is impossible to please him, for whoever would draw near to God must believe that he exists and that he rewards those who seek him."

Psalm 34:1

"I will bless the Lord at all times, his praises shall continually be in my mouth."

The Doors in Life

Doors in life open and close from time to time.
They either end a chapter or prepare us for a climb.
There are specific purposes and plans for us ahead
For God, our wise deliverer, has an underlining thread.

We're not always happy when a door gets slammed.
We sometimes kick and scream with all rationale be damned.
We haven't a clue that something better does exist.
And thinking outside of our understanding is felt to be a risk.

But God is all-knowing and has everything in control.
If only we trust in Him and let His plans unfold.
That open door holds blessings beyond our belief
And answers to prayers with paths leading to relief.

But we must have faith to enter that new domain
And not let doubts and fears keep us entrenched in pain.
To follow where God leads us and confidence He knows best.
That once we enter that door we're certain that He will do the rest.

I've stood at that open door too scared to proceed
When on the other side was all that I would need.
I pray for the strength to heed God's perfect will
And to go wherever He directs having that assurance still.

DRAWING CLOSER TO GOD

Having a close relationship with God is number one!
Oh, where would I be if not for the Father and His son?
Without them I am nothing, a shell, an empty vessel,
An ore without a boat and a star devoid of dazzle.

Believing is a choice and not mandated or required.
But thru upbringing, exposure and how one is hardwired.
I know not another like Him who is all there is to me.
A healer, a comforter, my protector who set me free.

I shall not bend any arm or push someone to agree.
May God's special light simply radiate thru me!
Even with my flaws and shortcomings He loves me still
And I do my best to walk proudly in His will!

The closer to eternity, the closer He is to me.
Lifting high my cross so He can ever see.
I dare not forget the many blessings He bestows.
Accepting me for me and shielding me from my foes.

He is my personal Savior, a mighty friend of mine.
The wind felt at my back and the fruit upon my vine.
The Great I Am and the hand that wipes my tears.
A Daddy who forever takes away my fears.

I Came to Jesus

I can't say for sure what really brought me to God
Or what became the catalyst or the lightening rod.
What touched my heart inside and made me repent?
What I was willing to do for Christ and what I underwent?

I always heard the word even when I drifted off or played.
I was listening to the messages some and as the preacher prayed.
I was a little girl who was quite easy to impress.
And I learned early in life to be obedient and at my best.

To Sunday School I went each week to be with other friends.
But tell me, how did I decided to turn away from sin?
I didn't understand all the clapping or the mysterious Holy Ghost.
But I enjoyed the shouting Saints and the singing the most!

My granddad was a church leader and often told his story.
Many years later I understood it and the full glory.
And as I took it in and let it run throughout my veins,
It hit a nerve and I discovered I no longer felt the same!

The God those elders praised invaded my young soul.
He isn't just for adults or offers salvation just for the old!
God began to touch a part of me and it cut me to the core
And suddenly I wanted to know Him and absorb the word more!

For months I fought the urge inside to get up from my seat
And grab the hand of fellowship and run to God to meet.
But on one particular Sunday I could not resist the pull
For I was overwhelmed and my heart was mighty full!

With tears streaming down my face I went to the altar
Not for form or fashion or to pretend or to barter.
I realized that Jesus saved me and paid a heavy price
For not only me but all the others there, the good, bad, the nice.

I knelt and gave my life to Christ and joy flooded me.
In that one decision sweet peace rushed in and set me free!
Through storms and on mountains I came to know this man.
He's the reason I'm here today and I'll never release His hand!

Romans 10:9

"That if you confess with your mouth the Lord Jesus Christ and believe in your heart that God raised Him from the dead, you will be saved."

HANDING IT TO GOD

Fill me up with faith, Lord, so I'm able to stand.
Help me to trust more as you implement your plan.
Take away my doubts and fears that I may honor you.
Place a song within my heart so I sing while going through.

Darkness is upon me, Lord, bring about your light.
Have your angels surround me in both day and night.
Show me how to avoid the crippling snares of sin.
Stomp the evil one and wipe away his silly grin.

Lord, hold my trembling hand in the valley below.
Be my guide and deliverer wherever I must go.
Restore my hope and passion that tried to slip away.
Lead with your loving-kindness and strengthen my vertebrae.

In your precious holiness, Lord, I can always confide.
To handle life's situations and remain firmly by my side.
This is my prayer and thanks for what I know you'll do.
I call the battle over now and that's all due to you!

MAY I REFLECT HIM

I hope when you see me you see the King
Like flowers in bloom indicate that it's spring.
May the works I do speak well of His name,
Be examples of Him and His word proclaim.

I'm just a vessel a reflection of Christ.
Representing the one who paid our price.
May my walk align with the message He brings
So I'll go to Heaven and be fitted with wings.

I'm far from perfect, just doing my best.
Learning each day through trials and tests.
Growing in strength, bathed in grace.
Washed in His blood and in spirit embraced.

I'm mindful of how I'm to tow the line
In both speech and my actions so as to align.
Placing my trust and faith in His hands.
Uplifting His goodness while following His commands.

LORD, YOU ...

Lord, you fed me when cupboards were bare.
Put a roof overhead when I had nothing to spare.
You clothed my children and kept me sane
And healed my body and soothed my pain.

Lord, you wiped away my flowing tears.
You stood right by me through all my fears.
Brought me through rains to bright sunshine
And led me when I was confused and blind.

Lord, you carried me when I was weak.
Heard me when I could not speak.
Covered me when I was cold and chilled.
Encouraged me when I needed to be filled.

Lord, you held me close as I fell apart!
You pieced together my broken heart.
You've been my eyes when I could not see
And remained a friend and my missing key!

Lord, you lifted me as I sank in dirt!
Comforted me when I was bruised and hurt.
Spoke to me when I was alone
And accepted me as your very own!

Lord, you meet my wants and supply my needs!
Come to me when I'm on my knees.
Take my hand when I need a guide.
Is here when I try to run and hide.

Lord, you love me when myself I can't!
Dispel the anger and prevent my rant.
Bring me joy when I'm down in despair.
Always show me how much you care!

Lord, you hung on a cross and died for me
And you've prepared my home in Eternity!
Giving more chances and forgiving my sins
For you know the true person I am within!

Lord, you are my absolute all and all,
The one and only I trust to call.
My breath, my life, my everything.
You wrap me safely beneath your wing!

Counting the Ways

Jesus, let us count your loving ways
That you bless your children's earthly days.
Though it is impossible to list all that you do
From waking us up to seeing us through.

You provide food, shelter and needs.
When others fail you always succeed.
Picking us up when knocked to our knees.
You're who we call with our constant pleas.

You give us hope in times of trouble
Even when we slip back into the rubble.
You never withdraw your love for us
Though we falter in faith and lack in trust.

Each heartbeat we have is because of you.
The breath we breathe is a special gift, too!
There is the use of our limbs, minds to think
And functioning organs operating in sync.

And arms that hug and hands that shake.
You are that clock insisting we wake.
We're able to laugh and able to smile.
You're with us until we go that last mile!

Granting wants, many just to teach.

Not to be forceful not to preach.

And the list goes on and stacks up high.

I can't list them all so I won't even try!

I speak for all whether near or far.

Thank you, Lord, for who you are!

If not for you then where would we be?

On a more personal note that includes me.

I Chronicles 16:34

"Give thanks to the Lord, for he is good; his love endures forever."

Our Jesus

He walked upon the water and healed the terribly ill.
He did this long ago and does the same thing still.
He calmed the ranging sea with a three word command.
This person I describe is more powerful than any man.

He started in a stable with livestock at His feet.
Kings from far away came to worship Him and greet.
After 30 years He prepared to go back home.
Lifted His cross to carry with not a single moan.

Those who chose to shun His words had ordered Him to die.
He hung upon a cross so salvation would apply.
The world lay on His shoulders and sin pierced His side.
He rose from a tomb and stretched His arms wide.

They remain open for us to give our hearts to Him.
To be with Him in Glory so eternity won't be grim.
Among the many miracles that He has left to do.
Is to welcome you in His flock because of His love for you.

Pray Daily

Prayer is essential to get through every day.
Don't start out unless you take the time to pray.
Because when you don't do that your day will be in shambles.
Girdle up yourself and don't take such a gamble.

When I rush about without giving God some praise
That has an adverse effect upon my day.
Things go wrong, troubles come and all is out of whack.
Prayer will cover even the littlest things and that is a fact!

God knows what's ahead that day: the things we do not see.
All He asks is to prepare for what is bound to be.
It only takes a minute to go to Him in prayer
To worship, praise and use time to talk and share.

Get the proper covering, be blessed by the King.
Make it a top priority with a familiar ring.
Don't chance it alone just open up each day.
Do the smart thing; make it a practice to always pray!

I'm Standing Still And Waiting

I'm standing still, Lord, and waiting for you.
I know you have the answer and know what I should do.
I've given it to you in prayer.
My faith is strong and I know you care.
Lord, I'm still waiting for you!

Calm my impatience, quiet my anxious thoughts.
Let your mighty power transcend my human faults.
I know that you are able and will come to my aide
And the storms and gales in my life will fade.
Yes, Lord, I'm still waiting for you!

In times of distress you have been my sole relief,
Slain my enemies and diminished compounding grief.
The walls of Jericho have tumbled to the ground
For your word and power is never short of your crown.
And, Lord, I am still waiting on you!

This is another chapter, another demon to slay.
I'm girdled up for the battle with you leading all the way.
You are never late for you're always right on time.
That strengthens my determination and reinforces my mind.
No matter how long, Lord, I'm still standing and waiting on you!

Through the Storms

In times of storms you bring me peace and calm.
You rock me in your arms until the light of dawn.
And when the wild winds and gales subside
You're still planted right here by my side!

No one else can I call on for comfort to lessen my fears.
No one else can hold me until there are no more tears.
All through the darkness you keep me safely under your care
And your love soothes the atmosphere and purifies the air.

When troubles like disasters appear to smash my world
And everything within me takes a dramatic swirl,
My faith and trust is tested yet you forgive my doubt.
Lifting me from despair and casting those demons out!

The friends I once could count on take a backseat
For you are here to rescue me so Satan suffers defeat!
If ever I face obstacles or slip into the valley below,
I call out your name, Dear Lord, for you are the pro!

Blessed is the day you snatched me from the sinking sand
And cleaned me up and cradled me in your loving hand.
And though storms may try to change my course in life,
I have a Savior who is the ruler over pestilence and strife!

Go Away Satan

As I talked with Jesus I sensed we weren't alone!
It was as if someone was listening to us on a telephone.
No sooner had my words been said with many thanks and praise,
I knew we had company trying to interject opposing ways!

But I claimed victory and kept on talking to the Lord,
Sharing my love for Him as we were on one accord.
I confirmed my plans to live by and began to put them in place.
Meanwhile, Satan was plotting to cause me to fall from grace.

Before I finished praising the Old Devil formed a scheme
For he did not want me to be happy or on the Savior's team!
He would do most anything to derail me from doing right.
Satan stood ready to see if I could really stay in the fight!

He heard my declarations of how I would succeed
And planned to underhandedly plant a different seed.
His mission was to stop me and make me eat my words
For faith is what I claimed and what he overheard!

I said I would not fold so easily or turnabout and run.
Satan doesn't realize that God has already won!
Each time a Saint decides to forge a holy walk
The Devil tries to interfere with his antics and doubletalk.

But I'm onto his devices and I'm aware of what's to gain.
My conviction will not leave me nor my choice ever wane!
For every good deed I attempt he places a stumbling block
By trying to shut doors and having them all locked.

But I picked up my cross one day headed for the King
And I won't be deterred by anything Satan attempts to bring.
He needs to simply pack up his toys and go far away.
I'm in my Savior's camp and I am darn sure here to stay!

James 4:7

*"Submit yourselves, then, to God. Resist the devil, and
he will flee from you."*

In Times Of Trouble

As winds of discontentment howl outside your door
And all you can do is pray and pace about the floor,
When pain attacks your body or troubles seem to last
Grip the hand of Jesus knowing your problems won't always last!

When others talk about you or put schemes into place
Or hills grow much steeper making it harder to run this race,
As burdens pile up and your way is not clear,
Our Lord and Savior is that refuge standing ever near!

Don't despair or lose faith by the struggles or the fight
For Jesus is the answer for your every midnight!
Just when dawn parts the clouds in the morning sky,
The same God who calmed the sea also holds you when you cry!

Like the waters gently lap the golden sands of riverbanks
We Saints trust His promises and in all things give Him thanks!
So, do not get discouraged or succumb in defeat
Jesus our advocator places offenders beneath our feet!

Ride it out with faith and your strength will be renewed
For God handles things when His own is going through!
For every drop of rain He brings rays of hope
And when we are drowning He is there with rafts and rope!

MORNING CHATS

Morning chats are soothing, calming, a must.
Receiving assurance from the deity I trust.
Thanking for another day grateful for last night.
Praising and requesting He stay with me in the light.

Recounting yesterday, the pitfalls and issues.
Knowing I have this Savior who knows just what to do.
Time spent in meditation and sharing in prayer
With the one who is ever present and shows how much He cares.

Receiving that feeling that concerns are in His hands.
Strengthened for the day for He truly understands.
Lighter because my burdens He lifted right away
So that I can worship Him and enjoy this given day.

Glad He takes my grievances and listens to me vent.
Blessed wholeheartedly by the messages He sent.
Peace is mine to have and hold and wear upon my chest
For my Great Jehovah deals with all of life's stress.

Courage And Faith

Courage and faith go hand in hand, one and two.
You have to have both to guide you through.
Stepping out on faith takes courage it is shown.
It's never easy to chance the next mile, the unknown.

Nervous and scared are maybe what you feel.
But somehow you gather your strength and wits still.
That voice which prompts you to move pass the fear
Says to trust God's plan for He'll always be near!

To leave a job or a home that you've already made
Or not knowing the future or if bills will get paid.
To turn your life upside down by way of a change
And hope that decision is worth the exchange.

With faith as small as a tiny mustard seed
We can move mountains and certainly succeed.
We are given courage not a sense of gloom.
Do away with doubts and take charge and bloom!

Courage is a mandate, a gift, a backbone.
Remember your faith and that you're never alone!
Step out on both with great expectations
For we are the products of the God of creation!

Be Patient with My Patience

Help my impatience, my want to have things now.
My habit of interference using my own know-how.
Putting my feet in things which are best left alone.
Getting in the mist of stuff just because I'm grown.

You have a timetable and things happen at your pace.
I get real impatient though I know that's a disgrace.
It seems to take forever and I try to hurry things along.
And that is how I screw things up and then they go wrong.

Teach me how to wait and not pull out all my hair.
Show me what to do so I don't slip into despair.
Remind me how you come through if only I wait.
For experience tells me that you are never late.

And when I want to make a move stop me in my tracks.
You are known to grant me what in life I lack.
For working on my patience is an ongoing fight.
Fix this pesky issue and please expedite!

I Believe

Some don't believe in God and think He's just a crock.
Perhaps they did not hear Him when He's stood and knocked!
Maybe they were raised without Him in their homes
Or haven't learned they don't have to face this world alone!

When they are sick and recover they think it just has passed
Or the medicines the doctor gave healed them at last.
After issues and hardships they praise their own inventions,
Not knowing those are due to God's miraculous interventions!

As problems, troubles and bullets were dodged,
They don't realize positive outcomes was Jesus in camouflage!
From the clothes on their bodies to the food upon their tables
Each item comes from God who makes all things able!

This includes our families and scientists and geniuses alike
And educators the world over and even those who act.
Those talents and gifts are much too numerous to list
And if it wasn't for Jesus Christ none of these would exist!

The change of seasons and the pretty rainbows,
Our beating hearts and air flowing from our noses,
Animals with their babies surviving day and night
Without having instructions and supposedly not as bright.

God hears our prayers and shows us the way

Protecting us from all harm each and every day.

Some call it coincidence or a fluke or whatever

But in my heart of hearts I know much better!

Others may not believe and that's certainly their choice.

But I'm a living witness and in Jesus I rejoice!

Without Him I'd certainly drown in my own sin.

So, thank goodness I had sense to invite Him on in!

From the stars in the sky to the mountains and seas,

All around us are examples of God's creativity!

Please, don't miss a chance for assurance and relief

For God is all powerful and in Him I believe!

Hebrews 11:6

"And without faith it is impossible to please God, because anyone who comes to him must believe that he exists and that he rewards those who earnestly seek him."

TROUBLES COME FOR A REASON

There is a reason for the trials I am going through.
They aren't to punish me but are examples for you.
Through my strength and behavior you get the glory.
I am the vessel by which you get to tell your story!

I think I'm weak but you see strength in me.
I feel I fail you but that's not what you see.
You have faith in me when I don't see evidence.
As I posture for the world it's me you must convince!

This revelation just occurred to me.
The issues have been so many that I could not see.
They are only here to prove who you are.
So others can see their issues aren't so bazaar.

They need an overcomer, someone who made it through.
In witnessing me they, too, see you!
Who am I to complain when you fight my every battle?
All you ask is for me to praise and stay in the saddle!

This hit me like a ton of bricks today.
All I need is to pray and obey.
From every trial I have comes something good.
Lord, forgive me for until today I never understood!

The Price

The price Jesus paid went beyond belief!
And hanging on a cross was cruel and not brief.
Even before He came to live on this earth
A plan was formed for after His birth.

They lied on Him and He went on trial.
He only wanted to save each person, each child!
They tortured, whipped and mocked this man
And took away His dignity and didn't understand.

We fuss about the cost we pay in the stores
But Jesus gave His life and paid so much more!
He did that for His accusers, for me and for you
To redeem us for the sins He knew we would do!

We aren't worthy of His great sacrifice.
Yet, with all we do He still paid the price!
Jesus carried His own cross and hung until He died,
Put up with abuse and never once cried!

They nailed His hands and feet and denied Him water.
He bled and suffered and became a true martyr!
We've been granted another chance by our Savior above
To repent for our sins in return for His love!

Sleeping in His Arms

Words are inadequate for what I must say.
Grateful to be given just one more day.
Having made it through another night.
As I slumbered I was still in His sight.

The world kept on spinning while I was asleep.
The stars went on twinkling and I heard not a peep.
My blood was flowing, my breathing just right.
In the comfort of a bed I awoke to earth's light.

Somewhere someone passed from life to death.
From a rising chest to having no breath.
They traveled from here to over yonder
To an existence where they no longer wander.

In a twinkling they traveled through a tunnel
Where time stood still and these years did funnel.
The colors of rainbows lit up that sky.
Discovering many answers during that thrilling goodbye.

Yet, I slept through dreams and visitations galore.
He didn't come for me beause there's more in store.
A universe around me claimed their own.
But it wasn't my time to float on home.

Thus, I am in bed just as before.
Rejuvenated and exhaling a snore.
There's use of my limbs and clarity in my thoughts.
Another chance to repent for all of my faults.

Guarded by angels and cradled in His arms
While He called others He kept me from harm.
So grateful my Father truly knows best.
Last night He watched over me while granting me rest.

∽

Deuteronomy 33:27

*"The eternal God is your refuge,
and underneath are the everlasting arms."*

HE IS MY SAFETY NET

There is a net beneath me to catch me when I fall.
The one holding it ever so close is who I always call.
Like a toddler crossing in traffic He takes and holds my hand
And if I tumble or hit the ground He lifts me so I can stand.

As the heat accelerates He keeps me from the flame
Preventing me from hurt or harm before I can call His name.
He is my great protector and my hero every day.
He watches out for dangers and hears me when I pray.

Momma couldn't always be here and Daddy was not around
But every time I need assistance My Lord can be found.
It does not matter what time of day or how busy He may be.
When I speak His name sincerely He responds back to me.

Now that I am grownup I know His strength and worth.
Thank goodness He has cared for me even before my timely birth.
People often fail us or make promises that they don't keep
But My Lord and Savior's on the job even when I'm fast asleep.

I don't take this lightly for I know He's granted me favor.
I try to show Him appreciation by my thanks and my behavior.
And when I start to slip again He gets me back on track.
And despite my imperfections He always has my back.

ALL BECAUSE HE CAN

Autumn has arrived with the miracle of nature's change
Painting an awesome picture with hues of every range.
Capturing the beauty that the season always brings.
Shouting the love which birds are compelled to sing.

A cooler sky frames the sights that take away our breath.
Kaleidoscopes of wonderment from a God of love and wealth.
Ushering in new hope and joy, a carpet to pave the way.
Ready for life's hibernation: a blessing out on display!

Every falling leaf a promise, a token of prosperity
Blanketing the earth so unbelievers have a chance to see.
Families of animals prepare for a winter's home.
While people face the evidence that we are not alone.

For man cannot do what this miracle provides.
We are not the artist nor are we qualified.
We are granted gifts and talents of different levels and size
But we aren't this creative, knowledgeable or wise!

I don't need an example to prove that God is real
Or to point out His ability or to highlight His skill.
This is just reminding how He is the great I Am
So others can grasp the idea and get with His program!

PICKUP, JESUS

Jesus, it's me, Lord, calling you on high.
I have my usual troubles and I'm trying not to cry.
Just a reminder I'm here and in need of you so much.
Please comfort and assure me for you are my crutch!

Thank you for the times you've put out nasty fires.
And when you blessed me with so many of life's desires.
For waking me up this morning and watching me last night.
Taking on my issues and manning my struggles and fights.

I hate to bother you again and be a royal pain
But I cast my troubles on you in your holy name.
They're too heavy for me to handle but you surely can.
You do what I can never do or that of any earthly man!

Though you're very busy in a world that's upside down,
Don't forget to stop by my neck of town.
In between your healing and blessings throw me a line,
Build up my faith and strengthen my spine.

Lead me through the forest; carry me on the beach.
Lift me from the waters and keep me well in reach.
Forgive me of my sins; anoint me with your blood.
Sprinkle me with love; protect me from the mud.

Thanks for taking my calls by answering every time
Even in my selfishness or when I start to whine.
I know you are caring for others and not just for me
And I appreciate your attention, your love and courtesy!

Strengthen My Faith

The preacher spoke a word from beyond the realm of earth.
It was a message I dearly needed and it caused a rebirth.
For discouragement is what I took to church with me today
And that weighed heavily upon me though I tried to pray it away.

When the word went forth it truly struck a nerve or two.
Now I am rejuvenated and armed as if I'm new.
Those moments of discontentment had really beaten me down.
And everywhere I turned more problems had me bound.

Today I took those troubles and tossed them on the altar
Knowing God's power would not fail me or falter.
I left the building high on God and refilled with faith and hope.
Now I can handle issues for I'm better able to cope.

I shouldn't break so easily or even lose my way so fast.
I pray God gives me added strength and that this time it will last.
Though life's arrows fiercely attack me please let me endure
For that's when faith is essential and I'll need it even more!

My Genesis

Oh, Creator of the earth, the land and the sea
Maker of all creatures, humans and me,
In all of your love, wisdom and humanity
You completed me with all the things I'd be!

Passion, caring, humility and much more.
A heart of love, loyalty and peace which you adore.
A willingness to honor, to follow, to obey,
A yearning for your kingdom which will house my soul one day!

Out of dust and a rib and the word of your mouth
From your spirit I was formed and singled out.
Stuffed inside with gratitude, appreciation and good.
Washed in your holy blood and before you I stood!

"It is good" your disclaimer for the miracle of that cell.
You nourished and protected me from the clutches of Hell.
I was born into iniquity, in shame and in sin
But baptized with your love so I'll live once again!

That was my beginning, a twinkle in your eye.
A speck in your universe, on an eagle's wing on high.
A tear drop, a prayer, the vein of your heart.
That stamp of approval you blessed from the start!

TEARS OF PRAISE

Liquid sunshine runs down my cheek.
No sense of loss, not sad or weak.
Rejoicing from the inside out.
My way of praise, an inward shout.

The word took over every issue.
Showed me God's love for me and you.
The more I tried to keep it in,
The more it rolled down off my chin!

Filled with the spirit, submerged in love.
Flying higher than an eagle, light as a dove.
Confirmation sent from Heaven's gate.
Learning the patience needed to wait.

My heart explodes as teardrops sting.
The voice of God continually rings.
Angels' melodies burst in the air.
The spirit, the passion spreading everywhere!

Pulse racing, all out of breath.
Nothing's in focus, a glance at death.
Grateful, honored longing for more.
But now confined on this side of the door!

When joy overflows from that sacred place,
It is seen in the tear ducts watering my face.
Cannot hide His goodness nor my gratitude.
What a public display of a personal rendezvous!

Sweet Jesus

Sweet Jesus, oh, lead me and guide me today.
Take control of my mind and show me the way.
Where I would stumble please break my fall
So with you I stand and can do so real tall!

Sweet Jesus, oh, hear the cries of my lips,
The pleadings, the praises, the songs and the quips.
And when I do err or be found doing wrong
Forgive me and help me obey and stay strong!

Sweet Jesus, oh, hug me and help me keep still,
To humble myself and give way to your will.
I just wish to serve you, to honor, to love
And someday go with you and live up above!

Sweet Jesus, oh, thank-you for all that you do.
So patient a listener and a mom for me, too.
I need you; I worship and glorify thy place
And when at Heaven's gate I'll seek out your face!

Sweet Jesus, oh, Jesus, I love your sweet name!
It is the one I call out to in sorrows and pain.
If not for your care and the power you give
I as a sinner would die and not live!

Sweet Jesus, oh, Lord for you I'll lie down
My burdens, my heartaches, the bruises unfound!
I trust in your word while offering you my soul
For you've sheltered me from birth until I'm now old!

Sweet Jesus, oh, my Savior in faith I adore!
Each day a new blessing making me love you more!
In sunshine, in rain and in all kinds of weather
Stay and protect me and standby me forever!

I Chronicles 16:25

"For great is the Lord and most worthy of praise;
he is to be feared above all gods."

CHAPTER 2

OVERCOMING ISSUES AND ADVERSITY

✝

Psalm 46: 1

"God is our refuge and strength, an ever present help in trouble."

Psalm 18:28

"You, Lord, keep my lamp burning;
my God turns my darkness into light."

Psalm 55:22

"Cast your burden on the Lord, and He shall sustain you;
He shall never permit the righteous to be moved."

ALWAYS HERE

You heard my first call and saw that first tear.
Watched as I knelt and listened to my fear.
You held me as the world collapsed about my feet.
And rocked me when I was consumed by defeat.

Depression and cares knocked me off my game.
My joy and spirit broke and life was not the same.
Your arms cradled me ever so tenderly and close.
The Father, the Son, the mighty Holy Ghost.

I bathed in your comfort, breathed in your word.
Regained strength by the encouragement I heard.
Took on your armor and was filled with your love.
Though undeserving of such care by three entities above.

Now I can stand and face my tomorrows.
I can run through the valleys and accept all the sorrows.
You're my safe haven, my hand when life grows dark,
My rock in times of storms and my patriarch.

You hold me when I cry, wiping my tearful face.
Soothing my heart and showering me with grace.
My hurts you take away, you minimize my fears.
My world's a better place because you're always here.

GRATITUDE

Another beautiful morning, another wonderful day.
Made it through the night and must take time to pray.
The sun is smiling down, the birds stoic in flight.
I thank God for mercy and for watching me during the night!

Warm breezes kiss my face, a song springs from my heart.
Gripping hold of reality for grace hit its mark.
Viewing Mother Nature's splendor as if it's in a frame.
Counting endless blessings which attest to God's name.

Gone the snow piles and the crisp cold air
Replaced by evidence of a new season everywhere.
Buds are awakening and so am I.
"Hello Spring" as I bid Old Man Winter "Goodbye!"

From the cocoon of my bondage to freedom at last.
The weather, the issues right now in the past.
All that I see is the work of God's love.
Spreading His wings like an eagle or dove.

Praising, rejoicing, appreciative of life.
Not focused on problems or troubles or strife.
Just grateful to live to love and to be.
And thanking God for these blessings I see!

In an Embrace of Comfort

Daddy, today I just need to crawl into your lap.
Hear your pounding heartbeat lovingly in your wrap.
The world has been so cruel and nipped harshly at my heels
And right now I need your comfort to calm what I feel.

The lull of your gentle tone, the rocking in your arms,
The soothing of my wounded spirit, the safety from all harm.
Just warm and breathing softly as the earth orbits around.
Sleepiness overcomes the person who slowly rebounds.

No motion is in the room. The light slowly grows more dim
As I try concentrating I slip further away from what I saw as grim.
Relaxing in thy bosom so relieved by your silent word.
Assured through your presence, cuddled as an injured bird.

Knowing all is well for my daddy is always here
Lifting me from all danger and wiping away each tear.
Sheltering me from the gales, the winds and life's brutalities.
My Father, the redeemer, the closest love there will ever be.

Struggles Make for Prayer

It is the troubles and pains that have made me strong,
All the potholes, the roadblocks, the frustrations the wrongs.
By every situation and valley and whatever I went through
Was a lesson learned and a closer step towards you.

If not for some issues prayers would've been few.
But with my inadequacies that's what I would do.
Crying and whining and begging you to come.
Overwhelmed, unworthy, looking crazy and dumb.

Because problems existed and fires would not cease,
I gained more strength and my faith increased.
It took all of that to bring me to my knees,
To kneel at the cross for prayer is the key.

A life supreme without problems or fears
Would not humble me or make you so dear.
There'd be no need for you or the use of prayer.
I would go about living with not a single care.

Yet, sorrows and heartaches are common today.
They always arrive but seldom do they stay.
The ups and the downs fill this juncture in life
And the world is made up of dangers and strife.

But these type circumstances lead to talks with you.
In prayer and with purpose you're here to carry me through.
For you are my Savior, on whom I can depend.
Thank God I had the sense one day to welcome you in!

Forgive to be Forgiven

Being Christ-like does come with a hefty price
Besides doing His will and behaving rather nice.
Our lives should reflect the goodness of the Lord.
The old self and sin are things we no longer can afford!

There is a certain way we are to treat one another.
A stranger is just as important as if he's a blood brother.
We are to love each other and let contentious matters go
By focus on doing right for the Bible says so.

Commit to solving issues and avoiding negatives is smart
For frayed nerves become much more difficult to depart.
Don't cling onto anger or the pangs of being upset.
Hand those over to Jesus and don't get sucked in by regrets.

Forgiveness is a gift to take yourself off the hook.
Regardless whose the offender or the route in which it took.
God wants us to move on and be the bigger one.
Forgive with all your heart and soul, be over it and done!

So, if someone has wronged you remember it'll be okay.
You have God's assurance and you're expected to obey.
When lies are told or evil deeds try not to succumb.
God will handle those, too, as well as the outcome!

He fights our every battle if we only trust.
Believe in His word and keeping our hands off is a real must.
Throw out all forms of malice, the grudges and ill will.
Lighten up your burdens and listen and be still.

Giving our lives to Christ guarantees a brand new life.
A Savior always to lean on, an advocate of strife.
A deliverer, a champion, a protector on hand.
A God who forgives us and who truly understands!

Forgive to be forgiven is a very fair rule.
If God didn't pardon us that would seem cruel.
But we are to do the same so He can recipicate.
None of us are perfect and need forgiveness on our plate!

Matthew 6:14

"For if you forgive other people when they sin against you,
your heavenly Father will also forgive you."

BEYOND THE FOREST AND TREES

We don't see what's beyond the forest and trees.
God does not tell us what is waiting and we don't see.
I'm the prime example when it came to being wed.
I had to wait over 30 years before God blessed my bed.

To me it looked as though I'd always be alone.
No interest in me and no man to put me on his throne.
What was I to think after so many lonely years?
I thought it wasn't to be and no man would ever appear!

But as I gave up hope and went on with my life,
God already had His plan to make me a wife.
I never saw this coming nor dreamed that this would exist.
Yet, in spite of the forest and trees God threw in that twist!

No one knows the future or what is God's will.
We may not see His vision but He has one for us still.
As we fret and worry His plan is being put in place.
We need to patiently wait on Him for truly it isn't a race!

So, I had to wait for decades for whatever reason why.
All happened for my own good and to that I can testify.
The forest and trees hid what was waiting just for me.
I had jumped to conclusions because my miracle I couldn't see!

Wait on God

Waiting can be difficult and our patience isn't long.
God's time seldom matches ours and His is never wrong!
The Bible states to wait on God for He is never late.
Yet, we seek immediate care and find it hard to wait!

He is omnipresent and is always by our side.
God has all power and His scope is unmeasurably wide!
There is nothing that our God can't do if it is His will.
And when He's ready to respond He can fulfill.

No amount of demanding or gestures of protest
Will rush God to perform faster to alleviate the stress.
He has the solution and knows when to put it in place.
Keep the faith and trust in Him for He has a timely pace.

We may grow weary and think that God will not appear.
That He has decided not to help is our greatest fear.
Be still because He's in control and always right on time.
The more you get to know Him the less you will whine!

Thanking You God

Woke up with a smile on my face and praises deep within.
How could I not be happy inside when for me a new day begins?
Some went to sleep last night and awakened in Glory.
God saw fit that I would live and continue on writing my story!

Have I done all that's required or lived a spotless life?
Are there times I missed the mark as a Christian or a wife?
Did I deserve to have the Death Angel pass over my door?
I must give God all my praises and do so a whole lot more!

When the world caved in on me God stayed by my side.
Even when I turned away not knowing He'd turn the tide.
I could praise Him night and day and never cover it all.
In spite of my neglectful ways He's here whenever I call!

No one in life has been this faithful and true.
Who puts up with my ups and downs and the silliness I do.
My protection did not stop when I acted like a dope.
For every issue I've had God has thrown me a rope.

That is why I praise Him and do the best that I can.
And when I fall short of this mission my God understands.
The blood of Jesus Christ is used to cleanse my sins and heart.
My love for God will not cease or from me ever depart!

Good morning, God! I thank-you for another day.

For bringing me through the night so my appreciation I can convey.

I serve you with honor, hailing what may come or be.

Keep me ever so humble and the cross of Jesus in front of me.

Touch all of us, fill us up and forgive us of our sins.

I pray for patience and endurance for any situation that I am in.

And when my time is up and I stand before you all alone.

Show me grace and mercy and welcome me on home!

I Thessalonians 5:16-18

"Rejoice always, pray without ceasing, in everything give thanks;
for this is the will of God in Jesus Christ for you."

MORNING PRAYER

While I say my morning prayer the past I recall
Reflecting upon His goodness and how He's my all and all!
Even when I sinned and strayed God was always here
Being the father I needed and holding me ever dear.

I made it through situations and came out rather well
Though I disobeyed Him and in His word didn't dwell.
There were times I called on Jesus and He came just the same.
Imagine all the bonuses when I stopped playing my little games!

Never was I abandoned and He kept back death and harm.
Even in my messes He kept me safely in His arm.
I did not deserve that and He didn't have to be so kind
When I was disrespectful, hardheaded and blind.

When I think of how it could've been I fall down on my knees
And thank Him for His grace and mercy and for loving me!
I was lost and confused and headed straight to Hell
Wallowing deep in sin and under Satan's spell.

God did not give up on me but fought for my soul!
I am forever grateful and now saved, redeemed and whole.
There is so much to thank Him for, way too much to say
For giving me this day but especially for all my yesterdays!

What a Wonderful Change

Change has made me smile when tears rise inside.

What a joy I have because in me God abides!

Change shook me up and conquered my sins,

Altered my desires and allowed Jesus in.

My destiny could not happen if not for change.

Salvation wouldn't be mine and would remain out of range.

It's natural to resist a new way in which to go.

God changed my whole life and for that I thank Him so!

My life changed completely when I fully accepted Him.

Now I'm not precariously perched upon a limb.

Birds are prettier, colors seem much brighter.

Food tastes better now and the snow is even whiter.

With Jesus my world has been flipped all about.

Just thinking of the change causes me to shout!

How I once lived and existed in times before

Makes me more appreciative and glad I don't anymore!

If asked if I want to return to my old sinful ways,

I'd hold my tongue for fear of what I'd say.

Only a fool would travel again down that scary road

And give up a chance with Jesus to be totally sold!

Just As I Am

With age, maturity and God I've come to a realization
That I'm ok just as I am and that's my declaration!
Always thought I was short of making the mark.
But that is a lie from Hell and nothing but a lark.

I'm okay! No, I'm the best and who God says that I am.
And anyone saying differently can just take it up with Him!
The good Lord accepts me with my imperfections and flaws.
In spite of any shortcomings He welcomes me with them all!

People may turn their backs or reject or loathe my ways,
Feel I am less than them or refuse to share their days.
But I have a father in Heaven who knows me inside out.
And He loves me just as I am and that's what loves is about!

Now who do I believe? The one without a clue
Or the God of my salvation who created and made me new?
So, others can go on thinking whatever they may.
I am grounded in Jesus Christ and I am exactly who He says!

ONLY JESUS

Only Jesus can lift the veil of shame.

Only Jesus when you utter His miraculous name.

It is His power that does the trick.

Because you are worthy He made you His pick.

Only Jesus feels your every hurt and sorrow

And is with you today and through each tomorrow.

Only on Jesus can you count on and rely.

He is your personal Savior is the reason why.

Only Jesus died for you and me.

It was His great love that set us sinners free.

Only Jesus goes that extra mile.

He even stood by us when we were lost and wild.

Our sins He has forgiven and thrown away.

And He won't bring them back up like folks do today.

Only Jesus can help get our lives together.

It is because of Jesus we grow and learn to be better.

My Gift to You

Lord, this is my gift especially for you
To do your will and what I must do.
Doing good deeds each single day
And taking the time to thank you and pray.

Telling of your goodness and sharing your word.
Letting others know your messages I've heard.
Taking a stand and showing through me
Your love and joy and the light of thee.

The gift of salvation and the work of the cross.
Thy way through you, Jesus, all misery to toss.
The road to your kingdom the path to your throne
Where sorrows are absent and hurts unknown.

These things and praise is all I can do
To honor and please and show gratitude.
The gift of sincerity to honor your grace
So I'll earn my crown when we meet face-to-face!

Praying for Mercy

The forest is sometimes thick and I cannot see.
If not for Jesus Christ, oh Lord, where would I be?
The more I try to find my way the more I am lost.
And if not for a shred of faith all hope I would toss.

Digging out one hole and another comes along.
Tell me God, my Savior, what am I doing wrong?
Every time I make a move down I go again.
In spite of all your promises I'm trembling deep within.

Help me, Lord, to hold on and not get off the course.
I know I'm being plagued right now by an evil force.
Though I trust in you and know you're always by my side,
I am weak and need your wing so beneath it I can hide.

Forgive me for the whining, the begging and the tears.
Take away my lack of strength and my battle with fear.
Direct me the way that I can overcome this mess.
Be my shining star to guide me through this latest test.

CHAPTER 3

A GENERAL ASSORTMENT OF POEMS

✝

Proverbs 3:5-6

*"Trust in the Lord with all your heart,
and lean not on your own understanding;
in all your ways acknowledge him and he shall direct your paths."*

Ecclesiastes 3:1

*"To everything there is a season
and a time to every purpose under Heaven."*

Matthew 6:33

*"But seek you first the Kingdom of God
and his righteousness and all these things shall be given you."*

Preparing for Heaven

The closer I get to Glory the less risks I take.
Heaven is my goal so all foolishness I must shake.
I used to take some chances for I thought death was far away.
But now I think of eternity and where I'll finally stay.

No gambling with my life for this journey is for real.
I want to see my Lord some day and be able to pass His drill.
No more fooling around and thinking there's time to spare.
For there'll be no excuses when I ascend into the air.

My age might have tricked me once but now I understand.
After hanging out with Satan in his frying pan.
But God took me back and surely set me straight.
He held death at bay for me and not a moment too late.

An angel I am not yet I try to do what's right.
I want to make the Heavenly team when called into the light.
My record might not be spotless but I'm giving it my best try.
We pass this way once and I'm preparing for when I die.

THE BLOOD OF JESUS

The blood of Jesus saves me from the perils of the grave.
He took the sting from death by His life He freely gave.
That blood He shed was so us sinners could find our way
If only we believe in Him and trust Him and obey!

He done that for the drunkard, the whore, the liar,
The adulterer, the thief and others headed to the fire.
Jesus did no wrong: no malice was in His heart.
He had a home in Paradise but came to do His part.

Was born of a woman and died by man's hands
Though He was ruler over Heaven and all earth's lands.
His blood flowed as the rivers to cover all our sins,
Atoning for our wickedness so in death we could enter in.

He had not a blemish or wrinkle to His mortal soul;
Yet, He hung upon a rugged cross so stoic and bold.
He could have walked away or come down and shown His crown
But He bled and died so we could be Heaven bound!

Did Jesus die on that cross in vain?
Are we worth His sacrifice and suffering and pain?
He forgave His executers: He thought of you and me.
The giving of His royal life assured us victory!

Honor Him with thanksgiving, worship and praise.
Live a righteous life on each and every day.
Tell others of His goodness and what He did for us all.
Be mindful of that blood for Jesus doesn't want anyone to fall.

REMEMBERING THAT FIRST EASTER

I see the blood running down the creases of your face.
A look of disappointment for an ungrateful human race.
The sight of your mother watching you suffer and die.
Those who saw your miracles weren't even standing by!

Remembering how you healed and the waters you calmed.
Knowing you would leave before the breaking of dawn.
Doing your Father's will for a world in disbelief.
Carried your own cross and then given no relief.

Shouts from ignorant men whom you came to save.
Grief and mockery was all they ever gave.
Last images of an earth you'd leave to travel on home.
Crying out to your daddy for you felt all alone.

Welcoming the darken sky and thunder that rolled.
Giving up the ghost for mankind's sinful souls.
No way for the King of Kings to make His exodus.
Yet, you sacrificed yourself for each one of us!

Today we celebrate your death in various ways,
From bunnies and candy to gatherings to praise.
New outfits and hams and making family ties.
All done in your honor because you died to rise.

Many lose sight of the meaning of this day,
Making it commercial and forgetting what you paid.
Because of you we get a chance to have Heaven as our home
All due to your loving act you so heroically did alone!

The Mighty Counselor

Sometimes you have to counsel yourself I say.
The proof's in the pudding; I did it today!
Besides God there was no one to share my pain.
Therefore, I write of the issue so that feeling will wane.

Because I'm a loner that's how it usually goes.
I write it out to Jesus the best way that I know.
He gives me peace and answers and His precious time
To work thru the problems and then I am fine.

I can then handle things better, smarter and wise.
Sometimes there's confusion and He sees my cries.
He is always near and hears my every pain.
With no one else do I ever feel the same!

So, I work things out with Jesus right by my side.
He is the only one in which normally I confide!
It's a lonely existence but what seems right.
How I manage my troubles whether day or night.

Jesus is a healer and definitely a way maker.
He is a good listener and problem taker.
He's an issue solver and a very dear friend.
When I'm all alone I welcome Him in.

Jesus is my counselor to whom I often call.
To sum this up He is my all and all!
That is how I get thru my really tough times.
And after He counsels me I am just fine!

SITTING IN THE PEWS

The minister is preaching and the spirit is high.
On a pew in the sanctuary sits a strange guy.
He does not say "amen" or with the choir sing a song.
Something about him tells me that he does not belong.

As we praise and clap our hands he does not even smile.
That is not required but it's weird after a while.
He did not pay attention and became a major distraction
While whispering, gossiping and doing stuff considered infractions.

His Bible was not opened so he did not read the word
Although I know he listened and that he really had heard.
Suddenly those around him began to fidget and talk.
Then one by one they got up and back and forth they walked.

They missed most of the message and he laughed with wicked glee.
I ignored his stupid antics for he annoyed and angered me.
When it came time for prayer and the winning of souls,
He looked around and glared discouragingly at such a worthy goal.

The last thing he wanted was another in God's book.
He spent his life conniving and doing evil was what that took.
His mission is always to lie and kill and even to steal.
And the last thing he wants is the progression of God's will.

How could he step within the walls of a church?
Pretending to follow Christ when all he does is sit and lurch.
Here saints try winning over sinners' tarnished hearts.
But he comes along to destroy individual apple carts.

He, too, quotes scriptures and knows what God has said.
He, also, is knowledgeable but wants us when we're dead.
The souls Jesus died for he wants below with him in Hell
And if that means him coming to church he'll do so and do it well.

Some Sundays he strikes out for everyone's on their best behavior.
But other times he wins a sinner or steals one from the Savior.
He travels to and fro to find recipients for his fire.
Claiming as many souls as he can is his greatest desire.

Today he was successful and he left rather smug.
He didn't have to work that hard or convince someone or tug.
Another in his column, another not bound for glory.
He think he is winning and that's the end of the story.

Next week he'll come again and lay in wait for more.
Hoping someone acts up and stumbles through his door.
But Jesus has the upper hand and the Shepherd gets His sheep.
Satan may fake us out but we're not always his for keeps.

Quiet Meditation

Bowing in deep meditation, lost in thoughts and prayer,
Just sitting on the pew alone and handing Him every care.
Recalling my week and everything that has occurred
While asking His forgiveness for not always living His word.

My heartfelt troubles tumble out and are stacked on the table
As I repent my sins and give thanks to God that I'm still able!
For life brings about issues and stumbling blocks are laid.
Yet, Jesus is my advocate and my mind on Him is stayed.

The service progresses; the choir sings an applicable song.
I'm caught up in my private worship as my faith grows ever strong.
When the minister starts his sermon I shove my thoughts aside
To hear the message from God which will help me on this ride.

Around me Saints come alive receiving their revelations.
I, too, am in the spirit and enjoying the celebration!
You may not see me jump or shout or dance about the floor
But the tears I dab from my face show I'm touched to my core.

I have invited my Lord to guide me through life's obstacle course,
To walk with me over hills and mountains and infiltrate my pores.
I thank and praise Him for making clear my Heavenly aim
For showing the value of His word with power in His name.

So, it's another Sunday that I'm intrigued by the Master's plan.
Knowing He has my interest at heart and I'm safe within His hand!
Time spent in contemplation submerged in deep thoughts
Praising God Almighty complete by what He's taught!

SOMEONE PRAYED

Someone prayed for me when I was out in the world.
They prayed when I was no longer a little innocent girl.
When I did not love myself some person loved me then.
Enough to go to God and pray about my sins.

Someone prayed for me when I went my own way.
I didn't have enough sense to even pause to pray.
I thought all the rules weren't really meant for me.
I was an exception and the truth I did not see.

Someone took their time and went for me in prayer.
I was living a dangerous life and had not a care.
I gambled with my life: stupidity was my name.
I didn't know how to come out of the rain.

Knees were bent in prayer and they were not mine.
My soul needed saving but I thought I was just fine.
I was kept before the altar; His blood covered me.
That's really how I escaped; that's how I got free.

When I did not pray for myself someone else did.
Prayers bombarded Heaven even when I backslid.
I know my mother prayed among those who prayed.
I was unaware although God came to my aid.

I in turn now keep many folks upon my tongue.
Just as others did when I was dumb and young.
Those prayers that were said did not fall on deaf ears.
Thanks to all those prayers I am saved and still here!

I Don't Need a Building

I don't need a building or any fancy pews.
No singing by the choir, no formal to dos.
A program isn't needed, no usher at the door.
No clothes upon my body, no greetings anymore.

All I need is Jesus and my heart and mind.
I can choose to praise Him most any old time.
I praise Him in the morning and throughout the day.
Any time I want to I can stop and pray.

I am the building, housing each single wall.
I carry God within me His great love and all.
This spirit I tote around; it's down in my soul.
He is a vital part of me which makes me whole.

I can dance if I want to or call out His name.
I don't need to practice and He loves me just the same.
In PJs I can worship Him or while on the toilet seat.
My hair can look a mess and doesn't need to be neat.

Alone we talk and while laying down I pray.
I can act as I've lost my mind and it's perfectly okay.
No one is in my business, no puzzled looks or sorrow.
God will be with me even through each tomorrow.

Renovating has me as a work in progress,
Fixing the nooks and crannies so I can be my best.
God is sprucing up my insides this I know.
And as He does this my love for Him grows!

At the Well

The woman at the well could have been me.
The image I presented was not what the Lord would see.
Just like that Samaritan my love interest was not my own.
I had settled for a man who I should have left alone.

It was just no big deal was my alibi.
But after I met Jesus I was aware of that lie.
It was a sin and persecution would surely be mine.
I drank the living waters so my soul would be fine.

That drink Jesus talked of guaranteed my eternal stay
Because I let Him into my heart on that fateful day.
Now I am redeemed and forgiven and a part of His fold.
Like the lady at the well Jesus restored my broken soul.

You cannot hide from Jesus nor should judge one another.
What you do in secret will not stay undercover.
A sin is still a sin and Jesus can't be deceived.
An encounter with the Master and deliverance you'll receive.

His Grace

Looking over my shoulder but there's nothing I see.
Sitting at the table no one else, except me.
Riding in the car, walking down the street,
Basically alone besides the people I meet.

Purse full of credit cards, my lipstick, a comb.
Whether in the store, at church or at home.
When I sleep or I'm awake or I eat, run or sit;
Regardless, what I do I always carry it.

It is weightless, odorless and completely free.
I didn't have to purchase it: it's been given to me.
More precious than gold and it's mine alone.
Can't measure its value and it isn't on loan.

No strings are attached, deserving I'm not.
It won't rust or corrode or break or rot.
This is given from God and not earned by me.
Even before my salvation it came with mercy.

From birth to now, without reason or rhyme.
Despite how I am it's here all the time.
I speak of God's grace that follows me around.
Protecting and covering all of my ground.

Grace is what follows yet leads me each day.

Through hills and valleys, in all times it's stayed.

When I was lost it was present even then.

As I wallowed in dirt and was bogged down with sin.

Grace is determined to be in my life.

It doesn't shy away from my behaviors or strife.

What favor, what love this blessing of grace

And I'm grateful to have it as I run this race!

II Corinthians 12:9

"And He said to me, My grace is sufficient for you, for my strength is made perfect in weakness."

Touching His Hem

Jesus was near me and I was sick and dismayed.
I reached through the crowd as I held my breath and prayed.
If I could only touch His cloak I knew He'd understand
For I'd be healed by holding just that fabric in my hand.

I never intended to cause a fuss or to stop Him in His tracks.
But I wanted Him to get the Devil off of my back.
Others were shoving and against me all was stacked.
I felt alone and my health was under attack.

I just needed a tiny piece of His garment that day.
Satan would be angry and Jesus would have His way.
Even in that pushing mob Jesus knew that it was me
Who touch His sacred robe and He healed me instantly!

Without chastising but using royal love and care
Jesus turned and greeted me ending my nightmare.
He truly has power that is off the rector scale.
By touching that teeny piece I'm on the Redemption Trail.

My sins were forgiven while healing occurred.
I needed thorough cleansing: I needed His holy word.
Those demons that chased me scattered and fled.
That very touch did the trick: my old self is dead!

It was worth pressing forward for this benefit.

All else before that day was only counterfeit.

Jesus came that I would live and He made me whole.

My name was written in the Book restoring what Satan stole!

I had faith enough to touch Jesus as He was going by.

Now He is my everything, the apple of my eye.

From filthy to spotless from lost to now found.

Because of His garment I am Heaven bound!

Luke 8:48

*"And He said unto her, Daughter, be of good comfort:
thy faith hath made thee whole; go in peace."*

The Ultimate Sacrifice

She watched baby Moses drift down the stream
To keep him safe from harm and achieve a dream.
He grew up to save his people so they would be free.
Carried hope and the promise across a desert and a sea.

Mothers sacrifice in order to provide a better life.
None want their children enthralled in any strife.
They often give up what they love the very most
And trust in a God who is always at His post.

God so loved the world that He gave His all.
Sending down Jesus Christ was a personal call.
He knew the fateful outcome and what His child would endure.
But that was exactly what Jesus' birth was planned for.

What will we give up to assure such good results?
Unselfishly donating that which can never be bought?
Giving until it hurts for the good of the whole?
Making it about salvation and what's best for the soul?

CALLING ON YOU

Calling your name is as natural as breathing in air
For I hold you in my heart and take you everywhere.
As the strong winds blow trying hard to topple me,
I automatically speak your name and suddenly I feel free!

At times my path is blocked with no way out in sight.
Yet, by just sighing your name a new route comes to light.
In those instances in life when not everyone will do,
Without a second thought I call upon you!

Many promise to always be near
But when they're actually needed they fail to appear.
I can count on you with just a whisper of your name.
While others often disappoint, Lord, your word remains the same!

As the dark midnights enter and stubbornly stay,
I have that magic potion which chases them away.
I go down on bended knee or behind my closet door
Or simply stop in my tracks and call on you once more.

For every single battle which ravages my torn soul,
I let your name be heard and again 1 am made whole.
Why test the deep waters or bang my head upon a wall
For I know who has the answer and is waiting on my call!

He Had to Leave

This morning I know Satan was made to run out the door.
Because of God's presence he could not stand being there anymore!
The spiritual choir sang that rogue right out of his seat.
Those praising in the pews assaulted him and stomped upon his feet!

The preacher got to shouting so and the message hurt his ears.
The word of Jesus Christ isn't what this intruder wanted to hear!
He saw no one whispering or doing things which were wrong
And he knew inside this sanctuary he really did not belong!

The spirit of the Lord was high and way too much to bear.
He needed to flee, get the heck out and far away from there!
He made it to the backdoor but the ushers blocked his way.
Yet, everything within Him knew he could not wait or stay!

The clapping from the worshipping Saints penetrated his head.
He refused the gospel because his heart is really dead!
And as he escaped the building he paused and had a last look.
He shook his head in disbelief at the names wrote in God's holy book!

His plan was to steal, to kill and to bring about confusion
But that was foiled on this mission and he then had no illusions!
And as he ran away he vowed to try again next week
After this flock has once more tasted the world inside he will creep!

He'll show up early and craft another strategic plan
Hoping he can dampen the service and outwit some mortal man!
No, this Sunday morning won't be his final chosen one
For he will not give up trying until his work has been done!

BATHING WITH JESUS

The water glides over my limbs and circles down the drain.
As I lather my tired body I softly speak His name.
My mind revisits those yesterdays and how I made it through.
And I think about my schedule today and what I now must do.

I tell Him how much I love Him and thank Him for all He's done
As I rinse the soap from off myself for another day has begun.
This is a time we usually talk and then I'm out the door.
When toweling off I pause my praise and get ready for what's in store.

When I step from out the shower I have voiced appreciation
And I've let God know I'm overwhelmed with gratification.
Sometimes our talks continue especially if I've cried
And I make sure He knows I always need Him firmly by my side.

After situations occur where He has intervened
Our sessions are extended as I tell Him what His love means.
I may not express my feelings precisely when my alarm rings
But during the day we often talk and at times we even sing.

In the car I continue to praise Him while angels guide the way
Because sometimes I'm rejoicing so that I don't know night from day.
My praising does not stop at an assigned hour
For I'm constantly talking, praying and depending upon His power.

So, from my tub until I return to the pillow on my bed,
My Savior and I talk and He's never far from my head.
Because He is so faithful I always hold His hand,
By accepting His wisdom I have found that He's grand!

STROLLING IN THE GARDEN

In the garden of my mind I walk along with thee
With thoughts of a tomorrow with just my Savior and me.
It's such a lovely place where peacefulness abounds
And the joy I always sought down here I can feel all around!

There are the most gorgeous flowers which I ever hoped to see!
They cover the entire landscape for as far as the scenery can be.
Somehow, I know this is the place where habitation once begun.
And I realize my reward lies here when my life on earth is done!

It's a beautiful garden all fragrant and with lovely sights.
Like no place seen before and it's the same both day and night.
I'm blessed to stroll with my Master o're meadows and hills
Experiencing such euphoria which only Eternity can ever yield!

I see lush floral vines with leaves eagerly reaching out,
Caressing me with tickling arms from every little sprout.
The poignant smell so fresh and sweet and curls up to the blue sky.
This glimpse I've been given is surely reserved for Saints who die!

Yet, I'm standing in Eden, a place gripping my very soul.
Nature's canvas fully decorated in such wonderment untold!
Of all my wildest dreams I never could have imagined this
For it's more than I could've dreamed or could've wished!

Upon returning to reality that magnificent scene disappears.
But it has showed me my future when Jesus reappears!
The mystery veil was lifted a tad and I got to peek within
And I saw the place I'll live when away from sorrows and sin.

Though Adam and Eve were driven out and had to leave it behind,
Somehow I know some day that place will certainly be mine!
It's a garden for new beginnings with peace and joy everywhere.
And I'll stroll it with Jesus thanking Him for His loving care!

Psalm 19:1

"The heavens declare the glory of God;
the skies proclaim the work of his hands."

The Blessings of Insomnia

It is often during that early morning hour
That I feel your magnificent power!
You lull me from slumber and suddenly I'm awake.
I guess sometimes insomnia is what it really takes!

Instantly I return from faraway lands so deep.
My eyes pop wide open and no longer can I sleep.
Tossing and turning are both done in vain.
I don't recall any issues and my body feels no pain.

After laying there awhile my mind drifts to you.
This happens rather often and isn't surprising or new.
I begin thanking you for watching over me that night
And loving me and protecting me with all your might!

Things from out of my past play over in my head
Showing all the many blessing as I lay there in my bed.
I see the many times you came to my rescue.
Without you Lord in my life, oh, what would I do?

The minutes tick away: time goes by pretty fast.
I come back to the present after reviewing some of the past.
Some days have been a challenge and they take a heavy toll.
Issues surface and at moments tears will roll.

I think, I cry and heartfelt burdens explode.

Through praise and worship my problems I unload.

You understand my heartaches, my dreams, my prayers.

You wrap me in your loving arms and take on my cares.

So, when I'm awaken early it isn't so very bad.

I know it's for my benefit and that actually makes me glad!

Meditation, praise and prayer brings me closer to you.

That means waking me up when distractions are few!

Psalm 4:8

*"In peace I will lie down and sleep, for you alone, Lord,
make me dwell in safety."*

Watching Over Me

Woke a little early quite foggy from a dream.
In the haze of darkness things weren't what they seemed.
Before I could shake off sleep the images became clear.
On both sides of my bed were angels sitting near.

I was not afraid and they were not in a rush.
Their loving faces soothed me and the room held a hush.
Could I be just seeing things? Was this in my head?
All I'd done was say my prayers and slept in my bed.

Maybe they were present to usher me back home.
Did God send them here so I would not be alone?
Their pretty smiles assured me that was not to be.
Something on my insides said they always sat with me!

Though I did not know of them or that they were there,
As I slept each night they surrounded me with care.
I heard of guardian angels but we had never met.
And they were there nightly I'm willing to bet!

But before I could speak or thank them from my heart
They disappeared into the haze in a quick depart.
I sat there thinking, did angels I really see?
Or was my mind still clouded to some degree?

Casting eyes to Heaven I knew it was for real
As tears of gratitude gathered and began to spill.
If ever there was a doubt it now does not exist.
God sent His angels and I sent Him back a kiss!

Beware of Temptation

Temptation is something our God does not do.
For years I had it wrong and this fact I never knew.
Our relationship with Him is based on love and trust.
It is the Evil One who plants temptation in front of us.

I guess I bought into the Devil's lie thinking it was true.
Now I've been corrected and it makes more sense, too.
Satan even tried tempting Jesus before He died.
He used every trick he could to get Him on his side.

So, if he would tempt Jesus I know he'll come at me.
Thankfully, Jesus handled him and opened my eyes to see.
We never can let our guard down for Satan may get a hold.
Temptation is a ruse or a disguise to capture another soul.

This is a lesson well learned and a clear message received.
My manual, called the Bible, said it so I believe!
Don't fall for those clever temptations which Satan comes to sell.
He's hoping to manipulate us and take us with him to Hell!

OUR FATHER

Chess pieces, paper dolls, puppets which He controls.
God spoke life into existence and assigned certain roles.
He created the heavens, the earth and the whole vase atmosphere.
Out of nothing He formed man and placed us all right here.

God made us in His image and filled us with His breath,
Determined our life spans and the day we'll face our death.
What a mighty God He is to plan and care for us.
And all He ever asks in return is our praise, love and trust!

God gave us a will and a mind to decide.
He blesses us tremendously while equipping us for this ride.
He's here to break our falls and to lift us from our mess.
And God watches over us as we tackle each brand new test.

When we stray a little too far or even lose our way
Or fail to honor Him or we're rebellious or do not pray.
God forgives our many missteps and grants a clean slate
While coming to our rescue before it's deemed too late!

Without Him we are nothing, just mere dolls upon the floor
With very little hope or purpose and nothing concrete in store.
He's more than just the alpha and omega to His precious seed
And as we grow in faith we find that He's all we'll ever need!

We owe our lives to Him and whatever His master plan.
He's with us to the end like when life began!
He's a mighty creator and is all-knowing and wise
When we meet this puppeteer we're in for a surprise!

An Observation

The tiny squirrel scurried across the soggy ground.
The only creature stirring that I saw around.
As it went along I watched it go up a tall oak tree
And began to relate what its existence meant to me.

Like the little birds this animal naturally knew what to do.
It survived the latest snow just like me and you.
When I am in my warm dry house sheltered from the storm
God is caring for them, too, and are also in His arm.

Nothing happens by mere accident or is not in His plan.
There is a design in place for every species in this land.
Just as God covers us and always does provide
For even an innocent squirrel He is right there by its side.

In sunshine and in rain or when snow is all a blur
God takes care of this frisky bundle of skipping fur.
The eye that watches me and has never let me down
Is a loving Master sharing the power of His crown.

A blessed assurance that not one creation is any less
For all under the Heavens are truly loved and blessed.
Looking after even a sparrow, a squirrel or flawed me
With lots of grace and mercy which He allows us each to see.

Church Was Calling

Skipping church today filled me with some guilt!
I felt I needed a break and stayed beneath my quilt.
The clock showed me the bewitching time
But I convinced myself that missing a Sunday was not a crime!

I turned over in my bed but couldn't go back to sleep.
I went to the fridge but found nothing I wanted to eat.
I turned on the TV but to my grave despair
For after switching channels I found nothing noteworthy there!

I took out my laptop to write a little bit.
Before long no ideas flowed and that led me to just quit.
I sat upon the sofa wondering what next to do.
Something inside said, "You should have gone to Sunday School!"

I quickly shrugged that off and decided to shower.
While the water ran I thought of God's amazing power.
He has surely brought me such a mighty long way
But somehow this morning at home I chose to stay.

I grabbed a towel so I could then proceed to dry.
As I wiped I thought of what I did and questioned why.
I was missing the Saints and the word which was meant for me!
Suddenly, I realized where I should really be.

Something stirred inside me and would not let me rest.

I ran to my closet and quickly began to dress.

I made it to the chapel remorseful and out of breath.

I needed fellowship to prepare for the sting of death.

No one can tell my story of how I festered in waste.

How Jesus saved my soul and covered me with His grace.

How He threw away my sins and holds onto my hand.

No one but my Savior truly understands!

Today as a leisurely Sunday was not meant to be.

God had a personal message prepared just for me.

The bed, the TV, everything made it clear.

I was to be in church today for there was something I needed to hear!

Matthew 18:20

"For where there are two or three gathered together in My name,
I am there in the midst of them."

Introspective Vision

Looking through the window observing the display.
Beholding the royal beauty of another perfect day!
The birds are all a flutter, the sky a powder blue,
A breeze lightly fanning and my faith again renewed.

Someone went on to glory and today did not awake.
But I'm blessed to be here and this wonderment to partake!
Many don't have homes or they're sick or can't get well.
I am alive and fed and have a place in which to dwell.

A squirrel scurries up a tree: I hear the passing cars.
Life has not been ideal and I bare my share of scars.
Yet, in spite of my shortcomings and the battles I have with sin,
God of my salvation has cleared the slate once again.

Favored by His goodness, blessed by His love,
Kept throughout the madness by my Great Redeemer above.
Just to witness His handiwork and breathe another breath
Is a testament to a loving God who's with me unto death!

That bee upon the flower accentuates our state
In a world of not our making and on a future on which we wait.
As the caterpillar crawls along so does my waiting soul
Prepared to meet the power who has all control!

I can't make a blade of grass or bring about the rain
Nor count the stars in the heavens or erase a guilty stain.
The rainbow is a promise that only God can use.
He provides everything as seen by all life's clues.

Today is a blessing; a miracle clearly for me,
A chance to give thanks that I am forever free!
Tomorrow is but a distant dream that just may be lost
For tonight my soul may go to the one who paid the cost!

〜

John 1:3

"Through him all things were made;
without him nothing was made that has been made."

Satan Does Not Discriminate

Who am I to think the Devil only picks on me?
No one is exempt for he hates all humanity.
Every chance he gets he comes at each one of us.
Trying to make us converts and win over our trust.

He knows our weaknesses, flaws and tender spots.
He is clever and cunning though real power he has not.
He'll dress up any situation and wrap it in a lie,
Take the good you have and laugh as you cry.

All are targets but Christians are a special goal.
There is nothing like claiming a once Heaven-bound soul.
He's tallying up his victories and scheming every day.
He doesn't let our love of Christ stand in his way.

He hears us when we pray or complain or lose hope
And interjects doubts and fears so it's hard for us to cope.
He whispers suggestions which are contrary to God's word
And will have us all confused by what we then have heard.

Time is of no importance for he'll patiently wait.
There is no hurry when he holds an awful fate.
He plants little seeds about using those we know.
And lays in wait watching as his harvest grows.

No person is too young for age does not matter.

His job is to destroy us regardless of our spiritual chatter.

No, I am not alone on the hit list that he has made.

We all need to stay prayed up with our minds on Jesus stayed.

Satan defied God and lost his place up in Glory

And aims to make that each person's sad story.

He tries to block our chances and quotes the Bible, too.

Yet, he already knows God wins when life here is through.

John 10:10

"The thief comes only to steal and kill and destroy;
I have come that they may have life, and have it to the full."

Jesus Will Be There

Where were you when my mother died?
I lost my best friend and, oh, how I cried.
You may say to me that you really care
But through it all Jesus was there!

Where were you when the bills were do?
I had no money and was going through.
You always said that you did care
But at those times it was Jesus there!

Where were you when sickness came?
The pain was awful and I'm not the same.
You promised to keep me in your care
But only Jesus showed up there!

Where were you when I was lost?
Couldn't find my way and hope was tossed.
You did not lend a hand in care
But like always Jesus was there!

When storms came and knocked me down
No one helped or came around.
I thought that you would offer care
But Jesus Christ stood holding me there!

No matter what the situation may be
It boils down to just Jesus and me.
You haven't given me that needed care
So I count on Jesus for He'll be there!

OUR EASTER GIFT

Celebrating the resurrection of Jesus Christ, our Lord!
Knowing He died for humanity is what is underscored.
Miraculously came to earth and His leaving was the same.
And He died for a world of sinners so Eternity we may gain!

He even loves the truly wretched and those not yet born.
He put up with the pain and torture and such unfair scorn.
Who would take a beating for us and bleed upon the street
To assure sinners such as I could inherit a Heavenly seat?

Knowing that He'd be hung and had done no harm or wrong.
Giving up His place in Glory was a love unmeasurably strong.
Was spit upon, mocked and none of that was justified.
No bed for His birth and a borrowed tomb when He died.

He came to save our sorry souls, to cleanse us, to guide,
To take upon our burdens, to heal and change the tide.
This day was set aside to honor His sacrifice.
To praise and thank Jesus for lovingly paying our price!

CHAPTER 4

THE SUBJECT OF DEATH AND POEMS THAT MEMORIALIZE

✝

Matthew 5:4

"Blessed are those who mourn for they will be comforted."

Revelations 21:4

"He will wipe away every tear from their eyes.
There will be no more death or mourning or crying or pain,
for the old order of things has passed away."

Romans 6:23

"For the wages of sin is death but the gift of God is eternal life
in Christ Jesus our Lord."

By the Bedside Waiting

Sitting by a bedside watching monitors and lights,
While minutes turn into hour and days into nights.
Waiting not for a birth so that rejoicing takes place
But preparing to say goodbye staring death in the face.

We come into this world alone with God by our side.
And when we leave this realm God's still our guide.
Watching this end process isn't for the faint at heart.
Though Heaven is the destiny there's sadness in each depart.

For we humans do not want to ever let others go
Despite their journey that possessiveness will grow.
It becomes all about us and our feelings and needs.
But this is the will of God and His comforter intercedes.

Here is not our final home but a stop along the way.
We can't interfere or make a life born of woman stay.
Just like the dying have no choice neither do loved ones here.
We can only bid them farewell and dab each falling tear.

In Time

If only time could be reset, the clock put in reverse
Before Death came and the funeral and the hearse!
When all was intact and tears were contained,
Family together and thoughts of mourning unentertained.

In a time when laughter seemed free and lasting
And love was handed out without even asking.
Back then these wounds of lost did not exist
Which turned loved ones into contortionists.

Where voices once in unison produce echoes
Bouncing off the emptiness absence dittos
To relive what was then and replace what became.
Saying and doing those things left not the same.

Oh, to walk those hallow hallways of yesterday
Encased in still moments once thought to forever stay!
Yet, time in infinity will on someday meet
Joining those gone before and us here to repeat.

Don't Be Sad

We think of memories and at times are met with sorrow.
Those who once shared our lives won't be in our tomorrows.
The axe of death destroyed that and took them all away
And that gaping hole of absence is what now fills our day.

Events we shared are bittersweet and are frozen in our mind.
Comforting, yet crushing, as they preserve that special time.
If only time could rewind and we could start over again,
The brokenness of our hearts would no longer need to mend.

We would hug those treasured moments and never let them go.
That would happen then with the sadness we now know.
Every time we met we would savor that connection
And use each opportunity to hold those stamps of impression.

Memories are the fiber that binds future dreams.
They keep people close at heart and near us it seems.
Though they left our eyesight and drifted away,
Their indelible spirits are with us forever to stay.

When grief interjects and memories clog the brain
And tears want to rush in and the unfairness will not wane,
The smiles and laughter mix with the seeping of the loss
And aching and longing for them is the biggest cost.

They'd want us happy and remembering the good
Not crushed by the thoughts or exploring what should.
Look at the fond memories as glimpses of eternity
Where we'll reunite with those we desperately wish to see.

BECAUSE OF THE OBITS

I opened up the obituaries and I read a few.
I couldn't help but cry as I thought about you.
My life is not the same: your face I dearly miss!
I no longer have you here to share with you a kiss.

The time has been bittersweet, your absence a loss.
The heartache's horrific and your memories are at a cost.
The hole you left is healing but only by baby steps.
Just thoughts of you today has filled me with regrets.

I think of all our doings, the talks, our walks,
Times of laughter, seriousness and even our squawks.
And how I was not ready to have you go away.
That is what I ponder as I think of you today!

One day there'll be an obituary with my name in print.
Perhaps, someone will review moments we once spent.
Tears may flood their eyes for what we use to do
And they may yearn for me just as I'm doing now for you!

There is a peace in knowing you're not far away.
Just over the rainbow and in nature every day.
Beyond all the aches and pains and issues left behind
Just knowing I'll join you when God says it is my time!

BEYOND DEATH

Tell me about your journey, the floating and the light,
The brilliant array of colors, the plums, oranges and white.
How is it to rise above the boundaries of earth
And go through the sky to a place that was once our birth?

Did angels surround you then or they sang upon the shore?
Were you overwhelmed by all that was obviously in store?
Did you see the awesome saints of Biblical days
And those who touched your life in other ways?

What is the sunshine like there where days have no end?
Do the trees bud forever and bow down for the wind?
Are the flowers always in bloom and angels just flying about?
When you saw our Lord did you wildly dance and shout?

Just how was it to die knowing here would be the past?
Were you scared or anxious or simply happy at last?
Was it such an adventure that words can never describe,
A oneness with the universe that humans can't inscribe?

Do you come to visit me or see me beyond that realm?
Are you winged and robed and just sitting at the foot of Him?
Is it all you ever dreamed of or hoped it would ever be?
Are there any clues or advice that you'd love to give to me?

I have these concepts in my mind along with my imagination.
I've formed a vision of many things out of my own creation.
I wonder if what you saw and do is similar to what's in my dreams.
Or is my finite mind far from it and not as I think it would seem?

One day I, too, will travel that tunnel to my destiny
Through clouds and an atmosphere to a place of eternity!
I'll finally know the answers if that is meant to be
Once I'm called by God to join Him up in Glory!

Revelations 21:1

"Then I saw a new heaven and a new earth, for the first heaven and the first earth had passed away, and there was no longer any sea."

CELEBRATING OUR DEAD

Sadly, a seat on a pew is found empty today.
During this last year God called a dear loved one away.
They are no longer here but such sweet memories exist.
Though absent from us their presence we miss!

Gone are their smiles and those voices we once heard
To a place on high ushered in by God's word.
They are sleeping in Christ, resting in peace
For they answered God's will in His great expertise!

The circle has been broken and so have our hearts.
Yet, even today these persons play a big part.
As we carry on today we take them right along
Thru this celebration and during each uplifting song.

One day a candle for us, too, will be lit.
Many here among us will remember where we now sit.
Our name will be written or spoken out loud,
Causing fond memories which hang on a cloud.

Dying in Christ Jesus means living once again.
History is being made and was doing so back then.
This flame represents these angels happily among the stars.
Who left empty seats but in our hearts they're never far!

TRANSCENDING THIS REALM

Through the tunnel of love go I.
O're the meadows, the river, the clear bluest sky.
To a land of mystery beckoning me near.
Singing and pulling me through the atmosphere.

Colors unseen on this earth before.
Excited for what's waiting in store.
Feeling lighthearted and free with anticipation.
Hastening to His throne on such a joyous occasion!

It is my destiny, my final ascend.
The journey of a lifetime, a circle to end.
The stars reflect sweet images and echo my name.
All has passed away; nothing is the same.

Beauty overwhelms the limits of my mind.
Defying these boundaries; no sense of time.
The warmth of love engulfing my soul.
Arms embrace me, gone the man of old.

Love overflowing, bursting at the seams.
Knowing it's real, no imagining, not dreams.
Welcomed with kisses of angels all about.
Home at long last; joy explodes in a shout!

HOLDING YOU FOREVER

I see you when you are so sad and blue.
As tears are falling down I hold onto you.
Because my face is gone doesn't mean more despair.
God and I reside with you for both of us care!

Every time you sob our names suffering painful grief,
I ask God to comfort you and provide you with relief.
Death separated us but just for a moment in time.
That hasn't erased our love and know that I am fine!

I'm a guardian angel besides being mom and friend.
Earth has no sorrow that Heaven someday won't end.
The heartaches that still exist will then vanish in His call.
Glory awaits your arrival and you can't imagine that at all!

Dry those tears from your beautiful face.
Smile for you are blessed to be under God's grace.
You will always be central in my heart, my child.
There awaits our reunion when you've gone the last mile!

Always and Forever

Yes, I'm in the wind, the twinkling stars at night,
The dew upon the lovely flowers, the tear that blurs your sight.
In the bird up in the tree and the rainbow in the sky.
I now live with Jesus and with you, too, so please don't cry!

I often see you longing all sad and torn apart.
Because of me you cry a lot and I stay on your heart.
If only I could make you see that I'm always there,
How I hold you in my arms and stroke your head and hair.

Those feelings that come over you when you call my name is me
For I'm forever by your side but in a form which you can't see.
The movement that is often caught by just a quick glance
Is me visiting you and isn't done just by chance!

I understand your plight and what my death has caused.
I never meant to ever hurt you or bring about such pause.
For you are my precious child, the best gift I received
And I am still with you if only you believe!

In the Flowerbed

Am I a flower out in the garden who God will choose to pluck,
A single one standing out among the brush, thorns and muck?
Will He stop and scoop me up gathering me with the rest?
And gently place me into a pile with those He's labeled 'best?'
Or will God just skip over me and choose another one,
Considering me quite unsuitable and someone He should shun?
He is known to pick those flowers which are pleasing in His sight
And not just any old flower that some view in a different light.
Some flowers aren't fit for God's bouquet, revealing thorns.
Or something made them less likely to adorn.
Yet, even during life's issues I still bask in His light each day,
Praying I make the gardener's grade and not become a castaway!
All the flowers which are selected have to be the very best.
I'm praying I am chosen because I've passed God's bouquet test!

Psalm 116:15

"Precious in the sight of the Lord is the death of his faithful servants."

THE CHOSEN ONES

Some say God has a garden and chooses flowers He must pick.

And the very best or the pretty ones are those which do the trick.

Or God sees the trials or how life has grown tough

And therefore, He chooses someone who has had it mighty rough.

It could be from some illness or a body racked with pain

Or troubles or problems attacking with little left to gain.

The valleys may have been too low or the hills too high.

Whatever the reason may be God will call us each to die!

Whether He just likes pretty flowers for they make a nice bouquet

Or they brighten up Heaven or just add fragrance to a day.

It could be God wants those flowers where they will look their best

Or simply pluck them up to give new life or grant them rest.

God sees beyond our sorrows, the aches and stumbling blocks.

He knows our fears, our inner hearts and all of life's hard knocks.

And if He picks someone to join Him up in Heaven above,

They've earned the privilege to be pampered with His love.

So, if placed in His garden or seated near His throne,

When God calls out my name I know at last I'm going home!

ONE OF GOD'S ANGELS

God needed another angel to join with Saints above,
Someone good and faithful and worthy of sharing His gift of love.
He looked upon this sinful world and saw an honorable one
And said, "My precious flower, come be with me and my Son."
He knew the cares that plagued you and saw all your suffering, too.
He called you to His throne for you'd done all He needed of you.
Your name was written down in His book for you were spirit-lead.
He chose beautiful wings for you and placed a halo above your head.
God has granted you peace and joy while giving you blessed rest
With praises for your fortitude for you passed His entrance test!
I know if I'm ever discouraged I can whisper a simple prayer
And not only reach the Lord but know you, too, are there!

෴

Psalm 103:20

*"Praise the Lord, you his angels, you mighty ones who do his bidding,
who obey his word."*

In The Garden

God chose you for His garden when life's issues were hard to bear.

He came to get you now because He needs you over there.

His garden was incomplete and He saw your beauty and worth

And came and picked you up and took you from this old earth.

He had a certain spot picked out to be your special place,

A lovely fragrant flower with whom He'll share His love and grace!

Without you the garden would lack its awesome look.

So, God reached down and chose you because that is what it took.

Our hearts here are broken and our lives will never be the same.

Though we yearn for you sweet Heaven you have gained!

Be that cherished flower which flourishes up above,

Sprucing up God's garden as you bring to it more love.

For when God was considering who down here would be the best,

He saw that precious heart of yours and called you to your rest!

And although we miss you dearly and the tears we will not spare,

We know you are waiting for us in that garden up in the air.

CHAPTER 5

THE GIFT OF WRITING

✝

Ephesians 2:10

*"For we are God's handiwork created in Christ Jesus
to do good works which God prepared in advance for us to do."*

Romans 8:28

*"And we know that in all things God works for the good of those who love
him who have been called according to his purpose."*

Psalm 96:3

*"Declare His glory among the nations,
His wonders among all people."*

Just Following Instructions

On a mission I did not ask for or desired.
Would never chose this but feel that it's required.
This started as a hobby, a pleasant thing to do.
Little did I know that the writing bug would catch me, too.

Tried leaving this alone but it always pulled me back.
There are words and phrases in my head for a fact.
Whether day or night or by pure happenstance,
I am compelled to write whatever my circumstance.

This has become more than a habit, a compulsion, a must.
Got to believe there's a reason and this theory I trust.
Because it is a gift it holds a purpose for me
And these writings are to be read and for others to see.

They uplift me in times of stress and heartache
And help me find solutions or decisions to make.
Worshiping my God is much easier on my part.
Writing provides me a genuine peace at heart.

Not sharing this would be quite selfish and wrong.
Putting these out there is where they truly belong.
Writing is my calling but it's not meant just for me.
After reading my poetry I hope you will agree.

MY GREATEST CRITIC

She thinks I'm a genius, a smart and brilliant soul.
Quirky and misunderstood, a kindred spirit on patrol.
I laugh at her opinion of the person she thinks that I am.
I'm surely no Einstein nor am I some innocent lamb.

She is my greatest critic yet the one who applauds.
Her job is to keep me honest preventing temptations of fraud.
Every work is closely examined by her own expertise.
Nothing is ever finalized until she approves the release.

She nitpicks and criticizes assuring I get things right.
Often I wish she'd be silent since I'm the one who is so bright.
Thus, I edit and reread and correct things once more.
I want this muse to be satisfied with this entrepreneur.

And though she's overzealous I understand her care.
She wishes only the best for me avoiding hurt and despair.
So, I follow her instructions letting her weigh in.
Even when I'm in doubt she is here to defend.

No one can butt in or interfere except for her.
I trust the advice she gives and how she will refer.
And I guess I respect her strong voice of authority.
I suppose I should since she's the ego who lives inside of ME!

FOR HIM

It would be boasting and bragging is not me.
Thus, I kept this hid from others: it was done in secrecy.
Yet, continually I wrote of my blessings bestowed.
But finally faced the fact, these were meant to be told!

"Who me," I asked? I'm no student of His word.
Choosing me is ridiculous and simply absurd!
I'm always in the shadows not out in plain sight.
Could He be urging me to bring these to the light?

I know that it's a gift, a talent from Him
Not just for my healing, not just for some whim.
Others could benefit and many need to read.
These are great fodder for sheep who He must feed!

God is my Father and I must obey!
It is His decision and I can no longer run away.
Yield I must do and follow His call,
Honor His wishes and share these writings with one and all!

⌇

THIS GODLY GIFT

You give words which I have to write down.
I'm amazed and surprised by how you twist them around.
They're fixed in my mind but things go another way.
I simply record the message that you have me to say.

It's no longer just a hobby but a passion, a drive.
This is part of why I'm still here and alive.
Someone needs healing, encouragement and love,
A means to salvation, a path to above!

To identify, question, reach out a lost hand,
Ask for mercy or comfort or have another understand.
I'm just an instrument, a tool for the job.
Together we function as a door and its knob.

Sweet sounds penetrate this spirit in me.
Words demanding attention ring forth in harmony.
I just can't keep them inside: I must write and share.
Someone out here is waiting in need and in despair.

I'd rather hold these close, my babies, my soul
But putting selfishness aside I do as I'm told.
Whatever may come, whatever may be,
I write for you, Jesus, for you gave this gift to me!

MY GOD-GIVEN GIFTS

I didn't ask to come here or to even be
But God saw fit to create and bring about me!
Before the start of time began He planned my life ahead
And during my parents' union He willed my birth instead.

For after generations I landed here on earth.
A six pound baby girl who is challenged upon this turf.
I never knew my purpose or my place in history.
So, I prayed to God to enlighten and reveal my gifts to me.

For we all have a job on earth we're assigned to do
And I am no exception though at first I had no clue.
For years I tried figuring it out and racked my tiny brain.
I wished mine was to sing or act or up in lights see my name.

That was rather silly because those gifts aren't my call
Nor politics or running things; no none of those at all!
Yet, every chance I got I wrote from my heart
And it wasn't long before I knew that writing played a part.

I am just an ordinary lady, a mother and a wife.
I have no expertise, writing primarily of my own life.
Writing awakens my very soul and is my true passion.
While learning about myself I explore my heart's compassion!

Following another's assignment was never meant for me
And soon I realized I had a knack for writing poetry.
In my thirst for life's answers I stumbled upon this course.
I give God the full credit with joy and no remorse!

I do not take writing for granted and so this has gone on,
Sharing God's loving messages with each new blessed dawn!
I write about my inner feelings and pray I do my best
For God simply uses me and He does all the rest.

I didn't ask for this talent but I believe it's for a reason.
He picked me specifically for this time and season!
In writing I offer encouragement and try to do what's right,
That others may see Him through me and do good in His sight.

My writing is truly heartfelt and part of my DNA
Causing me to tell of God's goodness every single day.
Yet, when I think of happiness and what pleases me the most,
It is to share this special love and of that I proudly boast!

I Am His Bait

God gave me this talent and He wants me to share
To tell of His power, His love and His care,
To give Him the credit and give Him the glory
As I explore life's issues by telling my own story!

It's not about my gift or that I strive for fortune or fame.
It's about what God can do to bring forth His holy name!
Because it's His will and great love for me
He chose yours truly as a vessel others would see!

Many doubt that God exists and others still need to hear.
He wanted someone who'd use words to make things clear.
I write about many topics to which many can relate
For I've been given a talent and I'm a part of the bait!

Usually, I write of my emotions or of problems or stress.
While ministering to me, I pray that others are blessed!
His goal is to reach people while pointing out landmines
And informing them that Christ is needed for those daily grinds!

So, I do as I am told and I love what I do!
I simply write of matters which personally I've been through.
I'm compelled to tell of God's mercy, help and love
And to always give kudos to my Savior up above!

I like to think there is a difference that I make
When others see my honesty and realize I'm not fake!
And if this gets people to think and open up their hearts,
Then I've done God's will by doing my little part!

It's not that I'm so smart or holy or carry much weight
Or that I'm spotless, sinless or I'm so doggone great!
But because I am just me and plain ordinary,
Perhaps some soul will listen and accept the extraordinary!

So, as I am healed and find answers to my prayers
And unload my heavy burdens along with my cares,
Just maybe someone else will be led to Jesus Christ.
After all each of us is His precious merchandise!

⁓

Psalm 66:16

"Come and hear, all you who fear God;
let me tell you what he has done for me."

This is for You

Lord, I hope I'm not too busy writing to praise.
The point to this is to tell how loving you pays.
Don't let me miss the mark by simply choosing words
Instead of sharing what really needs to be heard.

Getting hung up on punctuation isn't right.
The purpose here is to shed some Christian light.
Fancy words and rhymes don't matter that much.
It's being a good steward and presenting God's touch.

Lord, I want to please you and just do your will.
This isn't about me but about you, still.
Continue to use me for your glory
And I promise always to tell your story!

If I get off track please redirect.
These writings are so that you I reflect.
Yes, I have this gift you placed in my hands
But I'm to tell the world so others understand.

It isn't about me and my accolades.
It is about you and the price you paid!
Keep me focused and honest for you
For I am blessed and honored to do this, too.

There is a dying world out there.
Help me show them how you really care.
Remove my ego and any need for fame.
Let all of this be for uplifting your name!

About the Author

Gwyn G. Harris says her greatest accomplishment in life is her children and grandchildren. Family is everything to her as is evident in many of her writings.

She was born in a small rural community on the Eastern Shore of Maryland growing up among general laborers and blue collar workers, farmers and watermen. Her world consists of loads of cousins, neighbors and friends all of whom were like family. Church was central to her upbringing and played an instrumental part in her development. She was the oldest sibling in the home and blessed to have three brothers and a sister.

Although her family was average in means she was oblivious to any challenges that may have occurred for her parents kept her safe and provided for and that is all she ever knew. It was when she went off to college at Bowie State University that she discovered a big, wide world truly existed. She earned a degree in Elementary Education because of her fondness for school. The teachers had always made learning interesting. However, because a job was not readily available in her county upon graduation she went to work for the national telecommunication company at the time and was employed there for 30 years before retiring. During that time she had a family and faithfully attended her childhood church.

Writing was always a hobby and started when she could barely read and write continuing on even today. Writing now is a passion and most of her works center around God and faith. After years of compiling binders of writings she realized there was a greater purpose other than doing that and storing the material. Thus, this book was developed.

Gwyn declares that writing is no longer just a hobby but a calling that she is required to answer. This is her way of sharing, giving back and honoring the head of her life, Jesus Christ. Her poems are conversations with her God, dealing with daily issues and praising His name while telling of her faith. Because of her love for Him she opens up her heart and we get to peek inside it.

www.ingramcontent.com/pod-product-compliance
Lightning Source LLC
Chambersburg PA
CBHW031857090426
42741CB00005B/530